HOMING: POEMS

by
Emily Decker

PUBLISHING

Baltimore, Maryland, USA

Homing: Poems
Copyright © 2025 by Yellow Arrow Publishing
All rights reserved.

Library of Congress Control Number: 2025940594
ISBN (paperback): 979-8-9883176-7-8

Cover and interior art and cover design by Alexa Laharty
(Instagram @alexaelisabeth).
Interior design by Yellow Arrow Publishing.
For more information, see yellowarrowpublishing.com.

CONTENTS

Homing: Poems

MIGRATION

LOW TIDE

In the dusky hours, as the marsh and its muckiness
are laid bare, I sit in a cracked, plastic Adirondack chair and my sweat.
There's no way to escape the cycle of filtering the day's living
through the saturated peat, no way to hide
the dankness that grows heavier in the southern May-day heat.
This is how it works, how it has always worked:
there are no ports of call, no tributaries, no migrations
without the underneathness of the wetland's coursing exchange.

Despite my stillness, the creek bed begins to move,
exposed. Crabs and water bugs skitter. I try to be stiller.

But as the fingernail moon beckons back the brackish flow, I rise
and return to the old house and her spirits, welcoming
the shadows lengthening across the shallows,
like a bedsheet tugged gently over newly dampened skin.

DAFFODILS

After Louise Glück

No one talks about the long in-between.
Sometimes, even we forget what endurance is,

what it means to stay down,
curled in a ball of hardened memory,

regenerating with every tremor from above,
hoping you will remember and not pave over our air,

denying us our short journey, or yourself
the yearly reminder of what yellow is—

an escape from your own in-betweens,
when you are curled in a ball

on your blue dumpster-dive couch
forgetting what it means to reappear.

FLOWER MOON OVER THE WYE

For once, I turn
at the right moment
and catch the apricot fuzz
of light creeping above
the trees lining the river's shore—
the beginning of spring's
quiet denouement.

We don't know what we want
from this moment,
idling in a dinghy
named *Providence*.
Do we invite the inevitable
shift, change the pace
of longing, let the moon's rise
put us to bed, too?
Or do we suspend
our disbelief in endings,
and hold on to this threshold
a little longer?

Fullness has her say,
and I pull the tiller,
turning the reflection of the sun
on the moon's face
into our wake.

SKIPPING STONES

Easter Saturday, we sat
on the dock's edge—
siblings in our waning 30s—
skipping stones
and drinking Natty Bohs.

I said something like,
There must be a latent ancientness
in each of us, calling us back
to the surface of our better beginnings,
the ones before the golden ratio
and the crucifixion took over
all the art.

You hmm'd and reached for another
can and a smoother stone.

We were uncertain miracles that day,
counting our skips and the seconds
the cormorants stayed under
before they broke through the surface
to dry out their wings on the fraying dock lines.

HERON IN BLUE

Your time of day—like mine—
is when the light is low
and lingering like the final
notes of a strummed ballad.
Your hazy gray turns bluer
against the seagrass,
and I follow your arc,
watching you land
on an almost pier-less
piling across the cove.

The ruins speak to you,
don't they? I smile, mostly
at the irony of your sound.
A squawk, really. A reminder
that grace can also be jarring,
that sometimes presence is
more memorable
than performance.

HARBINGERS IN THREES

The bones crunched like the gravel and broken halves
of bleached oyster shells under my mud-crusted boots.
I didn't register the difference until I kicked a rib.

Some part of a small animal. Three buzzards side-eyed me
from the dead, knotted pine hunched where the road
meets the bridge. I nodded to them as I passed.

Days later, lying on the bow of a moored boat, I watched
three more round each other in sloppy loops before I dozed off,
rocked by wake and burning in the noonday sun.

ROAD-TRIP COFFEE

I drink your coffee,
and I see a mountain rising
in the windshield's horizon
as we reach a clear stretch
of road and turn the station
to something like alt-rock.

The radio static smokes
out what I've wanted to say
for a week—the words,
a little acrid. My voice
cracks into embers
that slow dance by you
and fizzle on a borrowed
sweatshirt I'll probably forget
to wash before I pack it away
and move on to warm-weather
clothes—lighter materials
that will breathe
and wrinkle with me.

Another sip, another song ends,
and I know this: next fall
I'll pull your sweatshirt over
my head and pause mid-inhale
in a long drag of us,
then pour a fresh batch
into the wide-mouthed thermos
I can only hold with two hands.

FIGHTING THE SUNDAY SCARIES:
A TIMELINE

seven minutes before my bath: I decide to take a bath because I don't know what else to do despite the list of not-hard-to-dos scrawled on three sticky notes stuck to my countertop // in the bath: I think about the flies I saw in a neighbor's picture window on my morning walk—there must have been a hundred, lying legs up in perfect dead bug poses—and I think there's a poem there but it's too obvious // also in the bath: NPR is burbling in the background, and I catch bits of the week's horror stories, now so commonplace in their telling that the words are darkly soothing. would we know peace if we held it in our hands and not in our mouths? // eighteen minutes after the bath: I'm trying to assemble a poem out of Edgar Allan Poe refrigerator word magnets, and the words won't come even though they're right in front of me: grave crepuscular raven / dream amontillado / murmur pale midnight / nevermore dread unseen dawn / fly

POSTCARD FROM THOMAS POINT LIGHTHOUSE

We've just tacked
by the old lighthouse,
and a yellow butterfly—
a cloudless sulphur, I'm told—
has taken up our southward course,
beating with us
behind the backstay.
The late July wind is light,
and we'll start the motor soon.
But I want to keep the butterfly's
company a little longer. Long enough
to send a missive on its wings
to anyone who needs to hear,
in a fluttered whisper on a cloudless day,
You don't have to stay behind.

P.S. I will write soon.

NAVIGATION

SLACK TIDE

Silt has started to film on the still
surface of the creek around my kayak.

I was so easily pulled in this morning—
each stroke of the paddle a courtesy.

Sometimes it's nice not to have a choice,
to let yourself be taken in.

Current-less, I wait up creek
in an illusory calm, imagining

under me is a tidal tug-of-war,
until flow relinquishes to ebb: *Your turn*, she says.

Impatient, I pick up my paddle just as
a heron glides over the marsh grass.

The waters begin to move again,
and my bow breaks through.

THEME ON A PINK GERANIUM

I was standing in front of the peppers with a cart full of $4.99 pink geraniums when I heard the whistling. I knew the melody (*a movie theme?*) but couldn't place the title. It got louder until it stopped beside me. I was holding a bag of shishitos, and the whistler was a white-haired man who seemed more cheerful than his tune (*what was it?*).

You must have been standing here a long time to have plants growing from your cart, he said. I chuckled as I continued debating the peppers. *Oh, I've been here for ages.* He tipped his head, pleased at my response, and wandered toward the citrus, whistling again. It wasn't until I spotted him by a pyramid of cannoli that I remembered: *The Godfather*. I suddenly wanted to ask him why. Why the love theme from *The Godfather* in a Harris Teeter on a Thursday morning? But I didn't see-slash-hear him again until I was standing in the checkout line. He was walking through the sliding exit doors, still whistling, toting a pink geranium.

WATER NIGHT AND NEGRONIS

Ice orbs clink against sweaty rocks glasses as I hand him his drink. He accepts it with his left hand—a collection of Octavio Paz poems in his right.

– I sang his words before I read them.

– Oh yeah?

– An arrangement of "Water Night" with my college choir.

– Let's hear it.

I play a recording as he turns to the poem, and the bittersweet dissonance cuts through like the Campari. I sit across from him, drinking in the sky above his face as the voices crash and swell into "eyes of dream-water." Two seagulls, "moon-led," swoop toward the horizon behind his head—brushstrokes against the dimming day. I wait for the last chord to clear before I stand, take his drink, take his Paz, and take him inside.

MORNING AFTER

it's just me   and some tulip petals
on the coffee table   wrinkled and fading

in a spreading pool of light
               last night they were   mostly fine

still attached to their stems   bending toward
the window   in a cracked blue vase

he turned the vase   wondering if they'd leaned
on purpose   or if I had failed to arrange them well

they moved on their own I said   then went to bed
          but the turning must have been   too much   for us all

so now it's just me   and the petals on the coffee table
and some petal-less stems leaning toward the budding sun

WINDWARD TO LEEWARD

Windward
It was the nine knots   and the tinge of fall
    creeping into our lungs   and the amber-y light
      and your slow grin
        that said,
        Face me.

      No Irish blessing here.
      I'm not even sure what there is to bless.

    The luffing sails and dancing telltales start to pull focus,
    and we tighten our grips
      as we trim.
        I pull my hair away from my eyes.

We might always choose the wind
over each other. But do we ever
have a choice, really?

Leeward
You take my face in your hands, buffer me
from all we've just undone and didn't say.

I know the words already. I could
write them for you, like I used to.

But we see the gusts approaching,
and you give way as I stand on.

RACCOON IN DAYLIGHT

We startled each other, but she was more willing to hold
our gaze. It was afternoon, after all, and she looked sick
with her tufted, rust-brown fur striped with mange,
her right paw raised in a half-halt salute.

We stood apart, frozen like three figures in a tryptic,
unsure of whether to step into the other's landscape.
There was talk of rabies and buckshot.
Nothing good comes before dark in this case.

I wondered if she was playing with the light, testing out
the changing warmth between the tree trunks
and overgrown underbrush. So we walked on.
Darkness would come soon enough, and with it, who knows?

Drowsy owls and red foxes, or a night when you and I might
choose to stay within each other's reluctance to look away.

PEELING AWAY

I've been leaning against my counter longer than I'd planned.
It always happens this way, when I see the mounds
heaped at the Saturday market and remember
how good the peaches were last summer.
The best peaches I've ever had are always last summer's.
I buy too many, then wind up here, peeling away
and re-looking up hacks like ice baths that never work.
What makes the difference anyway between a peach
that peels easily and one that doesn't?
The ripeness, sure. But could it be its resistance
to being skinned and handed to a toddler,
or preserved in a blue mason jar,
or stuck in a freezer for the aspirational smoothie?

No one wants to be cored to their pit.
Still, I resent the slivers of fuzzy skin
that cling to more flesh than I want to give.

SISTERHOOD

They say "when pigs fly" as if it's something impossible, fantastical even. But clearly they've never met my sisters and me. Our feathers are like parachute-silk propellers that grow from the twist in our tails, and we only fly at night, when our pig vision is best. Our laughter sounds like the clink of fancy wine glasses, and our feathers whir like the humming motors in bubble machines or on little boats. Maybe you've heard us when sitting out on your stoop or in your car with the windows down, when the early fall breeze skims your face and you remember, it's not impossible, not everything is beyond you.

FINDING HOME IN A VILLANELLE

i found it once between the creases
of a mirrored smile and ever since, i've wondered
if i'll find it again, but in pieces.

maybe i'll stumble upon it on a summer day as it eases
its hold. with an unfolding map, unencumbered,
i set out on a path found between the creases.

maybe it'll appear in new leases
on a life where the rent is contentment, rendered
in family recipes i'll make again, but in pieces.

maybe it'll announce itself like ice cracking as it unfreezes,
and, in the timbre of a radio-god voice, declare, *i heard
you and found you here, between the creases.*

or maybe, like smiles, it shows up where it pleases,
and no one knows where until they're plundered
old souls finding each other again, but in pieces.

yes, this is how i see us: standing in light breezes,
living out the days forgetting they're numbered.
i found you once between the creases,
and i'll find you again, just in pieces.

RETURN

HIGH TIDE

1.
Sometimes, when the tide is too high, you can't cross
the old wooden bridge connecting Cappahosic Road—
where a weathered sign marks a land trade
from Chief Powhatan to Captain John Smith
for two great guns and grindstone—
to the worn-down driveways and crop fields
on the far side of Fox Creek.
In family lore, a great-great-aunt took her life
on this bridge, but no one really knows how
or why. A loss in another time
when such things weren't discussed.
The part of the story I remember is she took off her shoes.
Now, on one side, there's a mud-caked crab pot tangled up
with the reeds and a rusty No Trespassing sign on the other.

2.
The Francis Scott Key Bridge sits
on the bottom of the Patapsco,
rocked by the estuary tides,
waiting to be cleared from the channel,
piece by piece. In a journalist's photo,
a 50-mile-per-hour speed limit sign stands
stalwart on the edge
of the snapped concrete and rebar,
waiting for headlights.
Why is it that once we're past
the nursery rhymes,
we never think about the bridges
falling down
until they do?

3.
A late winter's high tide has flooded the streets again,
surrounding our apartment building on three sides.
The lampposts cast a Venetian glow,
and two intrepid paddleboarders cross the intersection.
What if we've misunderstood the Flood all along?
Maybe it wasn't an expression of a Father's punitive wrath,
but a Mother's messy way of deconstructing our destruction—
her too-high-tide way of saying,
I will wash it away,
and I will hold it all in my oceans:
> *your chosen graves,*
> *your fallen bridges,*
> *your buildings.*
I will hold it all.

ODE TO GRANDDADDY ALOE

You were a gift when he died,
a potted token of life against death.
You've earned your name, time and again,
propagating into larger and larger pots,
giving parts of yourself to friends
in their own mourning,
forgiving my forgetfulness,
enduring every move.
And still, from the shallow wooden cask
you've outgrown again,
your speckled, spiny limbs dip down and stretch out,
ever ready to soothe the burned things:
the thumbs that slipped off the oven mitt,
the blistered noses,
the curling-iron-seared lobes.

May you outlive yourself by lifetimes,
storing up your sporadic fill of city tap
and regenerating from your hacked off stems,
so the next generations—or maybe just a future me—
can see what it means to grow out of our ends.

BALD EAGLE SIGHTING: FAMILY REUNION

Your nest was empty that day.
Four generations of us gathered,
the oldest, 93, remembered
when the looming white pines
didn't stipple the view of the creek
and where his father's old skiff
was buried in the riverbank—
but he didn't remember ever seeing a bald eagle.

I think I know why you stayed away.
Why perch above all the repeated stories—
the variations of depressions and drafts,
sibling rifts that never quite healed,
dried-up oyster beds,
mothers dead too soon,
and illnesses never named—
as the cast iron pot simmered over the fire
with the family recipe for Brunswick Stew?

But the next day you did appear,
just before sunset, gliding over
the York as the brown-gray river
raised its own white-feathered caps,
reminding us that you, too,
have fought to stay.
Now, even buzzards back away
from their carcass-picking
when you approach.

THE PILES WE KEEP

Days ago the waterline reached
where the old name tree
once stood. Now it's just the stump,
cut off inches below where I'd carved
my initials and a lopsided heart
20 summers ago.
In its retreat, the water
has given back the riprap
and meager shoreline we called the beach.
Driftwood sits in piles
along with beer cans and pieces
of floats and chairs—remnants
of warmer days on the lake
that no one bothered to take with them.

Today, it's overcast, and a few drops fall,
patterning the water's surface with circles
in circles that fade with their widening.
This is a hard goodbye.

Soon I'll walk back up the gravel path
to return to the sorting and remembering
that stretch each decision
until another pile is made:

hand-tatted lace doilies—*donation box,*
a silk Japanese flag—*Dad's pile*
of wartime souvenirs,
the ceramic angel mug
that survived every cup of chamomile tea
and too-weak coffee we drank anyway—
[we laugh] *I'll take it.*

But for now, I've found my favorite collection
of rocks facing the mouth of the cove
where I used to mold bird-like animals
out of clay-sodden mud.
Once dried, they would be displayed
with a grandmother's pride in the windowsills
until, one by one, they would crumble
and be swept up with the rest
of the dust.

REFLECTIONS ON A YORK RIVER OYSTER

1.
Was it Swift who said,
He was a bold man
that first ate an oyster?

I think it was a woman.
Who else could predict
the complexity
of fresh water meeting salt,
the burden
of filtering the bay,
the palate and price
of triggering desire,
and decide to swallow it all?

2.
Protandric, adjective:
having male reproductive organs
while young
and female reproductive organs
later in a life cycle
You know, then,
how to be everything
to yourself.

3.
Shuck is such a word.
You don't make it easy either,
do you—until you're pried
and opened?

4.
Our oystermen ancestors
lived by the tides,
like you and with you,
until you couldn't,
and they couldn't,
and the bay and its rivers
grew murkier
with your absence—
for a time.
But you've come
back to your beds now,
old and new.

FRAGMENTS OF A REQUIEM

For Pearl Pocahontas Stubblefield Decker (1885–1930)

ad te omnis caro veniet
unto thee all flesh shall come,
eventually, and for you, it was too early.
winter days tending the brooding house
chickens proved too much.
bracing cold into downy warmth and back again
drowned your lungs.
yet still the eggs hatched.

lacrimosa dies illa
that day of tears and mourning,
the lamp running out of oil
was the only sound.
the women waited in the kitchen,
the men on the back porch, smoking,
until you shuddered a final breath on the daybed
laid out in the living room,
wrapped in the heat of the Franklin stove.
the nurse opened the door, and they knew.

libera animas omnium fidelium
deliver the souls of the faithful,
like you,
who played the pump organ
             every Sunday,
who made your own winter coats
             with store-bought fur collars and cuffs,

who delivered peach ice cream to neighbors
> with a horse named Pet,
who walked your children down to the river wharf
> to wave at the steamers puffing by.

chorus angelorum te suscipiat
may the chorus of angels receive thee
in your blue crepe-de-chine dress
and sing.

pleni sunt ceoli et terra
heaven and earth are full
of both the dead and the living.
your children
> had children
>> who have children
>>> who are having children.
oh, that you could see us
and the bluebirds that have nested in the eaves.

dona eis requiem
grant them rest
and joy. surely joy.
and everlasting fun
and never a moment's regret
over what's been undone.
peace doesn't seem enough,
not for eternity.

lux aeterna luceat eis
may eternal light shine upon them
and those who are left and have left.
may the light be as gentle as the sunbeams
dusting the keys, now yellowed and chipped,
of your Williams & Sons piano
bought with cashed-in mail bonds
before the Great War.
it still sits in the room where you died,
and sometimes someone, in passing,
will press an ivory key or two and remember
that it still makes a sound.

BOXING DAY

After leftovers, we broke down the cardboard casings
of Christmas morning and carted them outside,
piling them next to the firepit.
The ashes from the last bonfire
had mixed with the Georgia clay
and frozen into a reddish marbled slab.

An army-green dog toy had wedged against
the cindered block, gnawed side up. A bad toss
after too much of everything, probably.
Left alone with the matches, I started with the smaller boxes—
the ones with bits of glittered tags, ribbon spirals, and reindeer
wrapping, Scotch-taped and still clinging to the seams.

I hoped they would burn differently, maybe with a pop
and sparkle, before the edges blackened and curled
into themselves. But the wind picked up
and carried them, smoldering, over the fence,
and they settled like gray lace shrouds
on the neighbor's holly bush.

Nothing went up in flames,
but I bundled the rest of the boxes
into the recycling bin anyway and lugged it
to the curb. Mugs of spiked cider appeared.
We circled around the growing warmth
and shifted from foot to foot

until we decided it was time for more—
more leftovers, more naps,
more wondering where to put it all.
I picked up my niece, bundled in fleece, chattering,
smelling of baby powder and smoke,
and I thought about the boxes,

what they had held—
slippers and bourbon and books
and dinosaurs and pearls and pink tractors
and cards with gift cards and all that was asked for—
and what they could have held or never needed to hold.
Burning them suddenly seemed like a better end than reuse.

The ashes would richen the soil and from it,
what better abundance than
spring's green onions and irises,
or summer's okra and cherry tomatoes,
or fall's acorns and squashes,
or next winter's holly branches?

But as we shuffled inside, toddler's mittens
scratched my cheeks as she pulled my face to hers—
sticky and sweet with a secret—and I knew
every box I ever give her must hold everything
and more
and more.

WHEN THE YEAR TURNS

We eat black-eyed peas,
collard greens, and cornbread
like good Southerners. My mother
has been soaking the peas for two nights.
Two nights are better for these, she says. I take note
and watch her rinse, drain, and pour them
into the crockpot with the leftover ham hock.
Seasoning comes next, but the salt must wait
until the end. I think, *This is slow cooking.*

The number of days I visit
corresponds with the number of items
gathering on the guest room dresser—
souvenirs of a decluttering becoming
a curio collection of me, my mother, and hers:
Baby's First Christmas ornament, a crystal decanter,
a pack of candy cane cocktail napkins, and one
surviving teacup from a '90s Dollar Tree set of six—
a gift from me on a 10-year-old's allowance.
I'm asked if I want a silver egg service. She has two
and can't remember why. We never had soft-boiled eggs.
I refuse it and the chore of polishing on principle,
knowing I'm only putting off the inevitable
until another ending. I think, *This is memory-cycling.*

The drive back north is a watercolor
of winter gray and ragweed brown, broken up
by blurred pops of crayon-colored highway signs—
exit-number green, injury-lawyer blue,
fast-food red, Jesus-saves yellow. I wonder aloud
what we think the ad spend on salvation is these days.
When we reach the Savannah River,
a fog hovers over it, wary of revealing
the silvery surface already winking its way through
the mid-morning haze. I catch a glimpse
of the current eddying around a grandmother of a tree
whose weathered branches poke holes
in the lingering mist. I hold that image
until we cross the bridge. I think, *This is knowing.*

BODY AS A HOMING DEVICE

I am not covered in ink.
I am stained with the skin of things.
If I were stretched like a canvas,
I could connect the sunspots and scars
between my tattoos in a meandering map
to nowhere but my own living.

I do not take communion anymore.
I do remember the liturgy
and how the wafer melted
on my tongue—a symbolic divine body
absorbed by its creation.
This is my body, broken . . .

I am trying to understand.
Embodiment is trending in all its forms—
embody, embodying, embodied—
on podcasts standing in for real therapy these days.

These days, I dream
of sounding like a sonar
when I detect the next wreck
and bring it to the surface,
adding another tattoo
to mark the spot
in an after-map of discovery
that I am
home.

ACKNOWLEDGMENTS

My deepest gratitude goes to the friends, family, mentors, ghosts, and passersby who—whether they knew it or not—encouraged, challenged, and carried me through the writing of these poems.

Thank you to those who read these poems, often multiple times, and provided their generous time, insight, and expertise:

~ To Ann Lewis, my bosom, sunset-loving friend and partner in chapbook writing, editing, and general word-loving. This collection would likely not exist without you, starting from the moment you finagled our way into David Bottom's graduate workshop.

~ To my Tuesday poetry group over the past two years: Kitty Davis, Sue Eisenfeld, Tamara Evans, Marsha Kessler, Ann Kline, Sarah Konsmo, Heidi Kranz, Ellen McCabe, Ann Quinn, and Madaleine Sorkin.

~ To Holly Avera, sister of my heart, who, for a whole weekend, listened to me read and ramble as I attempted to organize this collection.

~ To dear ones who made a special point to read a poem—or a few—or encourage me along the way, particularly Anne Breitenbach, Audrey Decker, Jake Decker, Robert Edwards, Nicole Hart, Heather Sauers, and Sonny Walden.

Thank you to the tremendous poets whose workshops and edits helped inspire and refine many of these poems: Jose Hernandez Diaz, Emily Holland, and Ann Quinn.

Thank you to the gifted editors and team at Yellow Arrow Publishing, who saw and loved these poems into publication, and who continue to do the good work of uplifting women's voices.

Finally, thank you to the editors and publications where some of these poems first appeared in earlier versions:

Bay to Ocean Journal, 2023
"Reflections on a York River Oyster"

Yellow Arrow Journal, Spring 2023
"Boxing Day"

Hole in the Head Review (online), August 2023
"Raccoon in Daylight" and "Theme on a Pink Geranium"

Campfire Stories: Chesapeake Bay, April 2025
"Reflections on a York River Oyster"

EMILY DECKER was born in Virginia, on the Chesapeake Bay, and spent her childhood in Ghana and her growing-up years in Atlanta, Georgia. She holds degrees in literature and secondary English education from Georgia State University, and her poetry has appeared in *Yellow Arrow Journal*, *Full Bleed*, *Hole in the Head Review*, and *Bay to Ocean Journal*. Emily currently calls Baltimore, Maryland, home. She loves to participate in local theater, sing, and sail. *Homing: Poems* is her first collection.

Thank you for supporting independent publishing.

Yellow Arrow Publishing is a nonprofit supporting writers and artists who identify as women. Visit YellowArrowPublishing.com for information on our publications, workshops, and writing opportunities.